The World Is Round

NIKKY FINNEY
THE W**o**RLD IS
ROUND

InnerLight
PUBLISHING

InnerLight Publishing • Atlanta, Georgia

Published in 2003 by
InnerLight Publishing
P.O. Box 57143
Atlanta, GA 30343

www.innerlightpublishing.com

The World Is Round
Copyright © 2003 by Lynn Carol Nikky Finney

ISBN 0-9714890-3-3

10 9 8 7 6 5 4 3 2 1

Library of Congress Cataloging-in-Publication Data
Finney, Nikky.
　　The world is round / by Nikky Finney.
　　　　p. cm.
　　ISBN 0-9714890-3-3 (alk. paper)
　　ISBN 0-9714890-4-1 (pbk.: alk. paper)
　　I. Title.
　　PS3556.I53 W67 2003
　　811'.54--dc21
　　　　　　2002015392

Original cover art: Lynn Marshall-Linnemeier, *The Cloud Gatherers*
Photo: Circa 1895
Cover Design and Layout: Roy LaGrone
Typesetting/Design: Lazer Age, Inc., Atlanta, Georgia
Printed by Darby Printing, Atlanta, Georgia on acid-free paper

Other books by Nikky Finney
On Wings Made of Gauze
Rice
Heartwood

*For the tender-hearted insurgent
Lorraine Hansberry, who
"finished my thoughts" long
before I had them.*

Acknowledgments

Kelley Alexander, visionary publisher. Mary Anne Adams, tenured professor of walking tall. Valerie Boyd, gracious editor. Lynn Marshall-Linnemeier, artist supreme. Roy LaGrone, cover design, and Lazer Age of Atlanta, designers of celestial pages.

Walter Mosley, for your generous over-the-shoulder glances. Evelyn C. White, for your Key lime pie. Kwame Dawes, eagle-eye African. Valerie Maynard, *RICE* warrior general.

Affrilachia and your flock of poets. Collette Strother, treasured homey. Claire Prymus and Lena Boxton, rock steadies. Yakini Kemp, soul sister and Daddy's girl #2. Cave Canem, Black poet community I always knew could be, would be, shall always be.

Opal Baker, for 10 years of curry and mango. Donna Johnson, jewelry-making bibliophile of Lexington. Iniva Ngaka, daughter spirit made of Gabon gold dust sent straight to my door. Stephanie Martin, lion-hearted gal of Sister Vision.

The Kentucky Arts Council and the Kentucky Foundation for Women, for a decade of boundless support.

Grandma Colleen, Grandma Hilda, Ma Bea, and Mama Gen, grandmother greats. Mama, for your warm plates of shrimp, grits and okra. Daddy, for letting me lie down in the long back window of the Buick, so I would always know the where of the southern sky. Chip and Jerry, brother duo and their families, and the wide sweet valley of extended kin, for holding me seven hands high.

The color orange for health and courage. Jazz, reggae, and country music for making me close the blinds and dance with myself when nothing else could fix me. The deep bowl of the Atlantic; sweet, sour, watery breath place of resistance and return.

Ellen Sumter, for our many walks to the river to gather the streaming light.

With clasped and grateful hands, I touch knees and third eye to earth.

~NF

Contents

"You might think that a straight line is the shortest distance between two points but a woman's eye can travel in a curved line when she needs to see something and somebody is trying to keep her from seeing it, her eye can travel in a curved line to get there— and she will get there."

~ Modjeska Simkins

The World Is Round:
the breast of the garment measured

I began this side of life as infant photographer
focusing with the moving middle eye, the round
umbilical cord, where it melded into the body center
like a vacuum sucking in the sights.

Not with any eye but with skin did I see this,
do I remember now, the skin can so remember.

This picture that I first took of touch, here in the
studio body of birth, first photograph of feeling,
anchored by something other than the liquid
albumen world where I had lived from the first.

Something round, made of me and her and him.
Something akin to one large ballooning finger, here,
at the full lips of my belly's button where I could feel
the warmth of food; milky brown thick sugar passing
from her body's oven into my own whole-wheat

capsule. Too quick and the vacuum cord yanked,
tugged me yet another way and I twist-twirled
around in my curved world, falling back asleep,
genuflected by her soft snaking octopus arm.

Only one hour old and I remember
unlatching my eyes to see the tiny incubating
opening where I'd already lived for a week,
the warm stale air pouring in on me, not with my
mind but with full body camera do I remember this.

The perfect circular opening, round just like the end-
beginning of the cord, round like the camera's eye
that I would one day accidentally flutter inside of
discovering silky stems of wildebeest poems growing,
sour sweet filigree weeds.

I always return to the glove of her body, the touch of
her chord to my middle, my middle to her chord,
that opening where I first fell in love with the breast
of the garment, first recognized what fit, though I
could not yet safely wear it down the daylight

street. I can't show you any photographs of this to
prove what I'm telling you is true. I am remembering
this not with my mind but with my body; the body
can so remember what long ago left the accidental
scene of the eye.

"A woman has to be a daughter before she can be any kind of a woman. If she doesn't have that in mind, if she doesn't know how to relate to her ancestors, to her tribe, she is not good for much."

~Toni Morrison

The Squatting Sun

6:38 flying east, I witness birth;
pushing out of the blushing vaginal rim

like some wide cherry dropped child.
All the colors that make red have come

to the only straight line on the earth.
Ghostly, I blink, my eyes tweak her nipples

she releases and the head does not wait
for my awe.

I thought I knew what red looked like.
Believed I had seen this daily drama before;

the earth in morning mother motion,
the first bowl of earth breath sipped,

but never had I been asked
inside the sun's womb so deep.

What I see has so much to do
with the permission to look.

My egg white eyes labor to midwife
this moment out all the way.

The baby day pushes clean,
a quarter rim of cherry spilled earth

lands in a head back wail
inside my ladling pupils,

the first rising brightness and its long
equatorial head bursts then crests;

new life passed
to a pan of waiting salted water.

Coda

We are four to a bed   So close our hips must come
with hinges   A ticking of brown family   Thrown
across the cotton and feather mattress of winter
Tucked deep inside the house my grandfather raised
up from the red earth straight into the wooly air

The black and white photograph isn't supposed
to predict the future   But my mother looks like my
unborn brother   And even at three I am different
My tiny Black girl eyes are a queer shade of green
At five my older brother stands there on the end
Already buttoned into my father's sense of place

We are so close in this cherry bed   Our lightly
touching hips must surely be hinged   Even the
children have them   Daddy has moved into place
next to mama   Mama has moved in next to me   I
am the only one awake   The only one with a wall
The whole house has fallen   The movie begins

Uncle Billy is just home from Vietnam   He is the
baby   In the ruddy speckled flicker he stands before
us with a new camera that the war bought for him
I call Uncle Billy *The Bonneville Man*   Just like Pop
Leo he can fix anything   Unlike him he will only
drive a car if it's long and pretty

Thirty years later *The Bonneville Man* will die with
AIDS   Alone in another bed without hinges   A
dozen headlights polka dot the night screen wall
Every long pretty car he ever owned drives by to pay
their last respects   He snaps the picture of us all
Horns blow out in a scatter like blue Cadillac whales

We are a charm bracelet of a family bedding down
for the night   We are in the outback of my mother's
country   We have been laid flat for the sake of
photography   The elder aborigines bump room-to-rafter
watching us amazed   They whisper how much
we resemble early black and white T.V.

By midnight more of us have joined more of us   We
lop around the old four poster in a three-dimensional
ring like a Black family cut-out doll   We are joined at
the hip inside the old home house   We have been
hinged together in a place pulled from the red ribs
of ancient Indian land   Newberry

We are Southern North American Africans   When
we sleep together the rubbing of our bones makes for
a better crop   Daddy's hip bone click-clacks into
place next to Mama   And a new brother seven years
ten pounds and eight ounces away from birth
snuggles in next to me

The new tenant brother takes up space I thought was
all mine   But Mama says not to move him   She says
he's the last one   She says he will always need more
of her   The Silver Queen has already been harvested
The second reel begins

Down the road somebody passes a new baby over
a new grave freshly packed with sea shells   The
simmering dust spins off the blue corn silk   The
ochre wind patty-cakes the glass until dawn   I know
better than to sing along   Mama would only turn
and shush me   Tell me to stop playing with myself

This is why I always sleep by the wall   For company
So the movie will always have a screen   So the
screen will always have a witness   Now all I have to
do is live   Big brother there on the end turns   I follow
tumbling in an arc of bones   Our hinges shift
but never release   My feet and body begin to rise   I
leave the floor without warning

There is a white dog out in the woods howling
Pop Leo will shoot him between the eyes
tomorrow then drag him back to the clearing near
the arrowhead ground   He will never explain to me
what madness is and how we all can go

I am the only one awake to see the end   For twenty
years something or someone will come and lift me to
the ceiling and back whenever it wishes   I will come
to know this as brown girl levitation

The black snakes are tunneling under the hay in the
barn for warmth   I see the mice go still in terror at
the long dragon vessels nearing   They are born
knowing they can be swallowed whole   Like them
I have wondered how long it takes to die when you
are eaten and made to watch

I am counting   Practicing my numbers   At the cow
trough that Pop built fifty years ago with heavy two-
handed pieces of limestone   The spigot is dripping
nineteen drops per minute   Eleven Twelve Fifteen
I work hard on learning my numbers in case there is
ever a test   The water drips all night   Even though
I used two hands to shut it off like I was told

Except for the howling of something white farther off
in the woods that has lost someone it resembles   I
am attached at the waist to my brothers by my mother
but I know I am free to fly   I am a lee little long
legged girl   A southern mixture of red velvet rice
and everything nice   I have no memory of winter as
a child

A peacock is still something I have never seen before
But in two hours over breakfast Aunt Willa will lie
and say she has   Her sapphire words will glitter like
a tickling rain rolling off the curly tin roof of the barn
where mama used to dry apples as a girl   I will see
Aunt Willa's saucy words leave her mouth and hit
the frying air like that of a howling dog or a
torpedoing snake

I will remember last spring at the county fair when
Aunt Willa slithered toward us waving her turquoise
green tongue like a fan of exotic feathers   I do not
remember if Daddy snored back when we slept in
this warm ring of soft brown bones   And only now
do I understand that my random levitations and
landings had everything to do with four little girls
from Birmingham and a bomb

The all night rubbing of bones has turned the inside
tips of my fingers alabaster   The homemade cotton
sheets have been dusted on both sides with self-rising
flour   I need help hearing the many broken
whispers coming through the walls up from the land
The dead skin of my grandfather dropped for years
into this dirt like drum and bugle seed   Back then I
believed bombs came wrapped in Black churches

I always wanted a sister   Another girl to remember
the land   Another girl to help rewind the film back
onto the reel   Like shelves of brown Brittanica Pop
Leo's arms always knew the answer to everything
No visible time pieces were ever kept in this house
that he built and she made   So we would never
think of leaving

Any minute I will smell her perfect fig biscuits being
pulled from the wood-burning stove   He will pour
his black coffee out his cup and into his saucer   He
will drop his full Cherokee lips to the cool of the rim
He will tilt himself back into a sip so long it seems to
pray   As the baby light comes inviting the day I will
hear him wishing his throat was a mile long   Finally
I am falling asleep

I am the only girl   I know the hinges we have worn
all night made of soft shell salmon bones will fall
away at the first shock of light   I know when the red
rooster finally steps it will be like High John the
Conqueror into the morning broom-swept yard

Only then   Will we unhook as a mule team from the
gingerbread night   Only then   Will we one by one
make our way into the icebox bathroom   Only then
In the face bowl will the image appear   We will then
wash our privates by ourselves

The New Medicine

Evening

I go home just to touch them.

Rent a car that is newer than my own
for the long drive there,
to be sure I arrive without delay.

First the purple Tennessee mountains
blur the wide hips of the windshield,
then the blue tarheeled air
pours a southern smelling salt across my skin.

On the pedal my foot feels relentless,
I take the eight hours in one bite.
Before long the fat 500 miles
eat all the sun out the sky.

I am left a mere daughter
driving on sheer blacktop desire
to put my hands on them again.

That night I slump,
in a mother-daughter nest of repose,
repossessed once again
on her loud flowery couch.

My long fingers, delirious, spread,
lost in between her bare brown feet
that underneath are sleeping jellyfish,
on top squirming fiddler crabs.

She talks and I stare, the garden
of tiny lines around her mouth,
new rows, new rosebuds, in but a month.

I finger every bunion I can find
lingering pumpkin prayers in between
the smooth hollows of a foot
belonging to us both.

I never drive home to see them,
never arrive anxious to twist toward
their echoing laughter,
I travel mile after mile just to touch them.

Morning

I could find him in my sleep if I had to
but I only have to push the screen
to enter my father's morning territory.

One tiny acre of back porch land
where he always sits in the last
of the earth's night melanin.

He and his companion cigarettes have spent
fifty years of mornings together,
his sweet morning raspiness as predictable
as Sunday morning salmon and grits.

My fingers move like a honeyed light
for the back of his head. I move in behind his chair,
reach-draping my arms across his chest.
Bending, I berth his cheek with mine.

Our father-daughter chin hairs
ying-yang graze, like two of the same kind
of cat. My hands fold, braid out across his chest,
in an old sweetgrass weave, that if unraveled
would spill the story: How we own each other's
heart.

I lean back into the wall, one hand falls down loose
across his neck bone, the other takes to his jaw and
stays, rubbing his prickly chin there until the sun
brilliantly permissions me to go.

Twilight

I go home just to touch them.

Their black crystal lives genie rub against me,
polishing. Long before reports appeared of touch
being the new medicine of the new millennium.

Before touch suddenly became in and all the rage,
moving in beside Echinacea and New Age healing.
Before they invested millions in New England clinical
trials, needing to study it all up close.

Before handing puppies to prisoners as salvation
and kittens to old folks in nursing homes. Before
telephone commercials sold everyone on the many
intrinsic benefits of it and long distance.

By camel, bus, train or foot; I traveled.
My empty hands begging, breathless,
twin compasses spinning before me
for the unpanned gold of their skin.

For the oldest brother's patty-cake back hug,
for the youngest's full lip kiss,
for my grandmother's forward bent body
pushed snug into my waist

Days later I find her still there. In the bog
of the bathroom mirror, pushed so tight,
her silhouette still floating, still cameoed
just above my navel.

I never drive to see them. Never drive to
listen as they whisper and shout my name.
But I will do anything just to touch them.

My hands renamed Caseopia, fraternal lanterns
of every seafaring daughter, clothed in her
gauzy winding memory paper, she always
pointing out to me the copper coordinates
of wherever they may be.

Lobengula: her wall-bound child

Behind my side of the headboard
my son sleeps with me,
both eyes frozen open
all through the night.

When I make queensize love
in a woman's pot of heat
or dream a fetal curl around
a word, frenzied to finalize a line,
his glass-housed body
tap-taps against the wall.

His brown ocean face
becomes a dandelion tree
and I blow him around
with my eyes,
seeds fly between us.

We scandalize the room,
his tiny invisible voice
always the pollinating one,
Mommy, you're trying too hard again.

Each time he opens his floating
mouth a black bunched web
of his boyish silk skates across
the air, my new mother's netting
stretches out to hold, fragile
as ten teacups full of a baby's
first breath.

Lobengula has my ropey hair,
my spacey teeth, my love for precision,
but wears someone else's tentative smile,
looking something but nothing like me,
all at once.

He is a found-child, in an airport
gift shop in Kingston, covered in island
sugar cane dust then mailed to me
duty free way back across the water.

He arrived with gift card still tied to his
framed wrists. A nametag whispering
on a summer train, child on the move
between families,
And you thought you'd never have a son. Love, Lorna

He is all the brown face boy
I will ever have.
All I will ever nail
Jesus-high into a birth wall.

I have missed ever knowing him,
missed marking his height off
on the kitchen wall, lip kissing
my morning worry
into the mitt of his hand,
shining my nose into his sleeping
high school breath in search of homemade
wine guzzled, he finally confesses,
in the bus lot between state championship quarters.

"Who is that?" Wanderers to the bedroom
want to know.

"That is my son. He lives behind me
where I sleep. He is a wall-bound child."

"What is a wall-bound child? And when
did you have one?"

"It means if he leaves the air in this room
he will die without me."

"But he is too big to still sleep with his mother.
What will people say?"

"They will say I am unfit to have a son that
can never leave his mother's room."

But they will be so wrong.

Mean Nina

Lying there in state when I arrive
is great aunt Nina.

Nina of the Pear Gum trees, of the old old ways.
Seamstress of flowers so fine, thread laid to silken
seed, inside the eyelids of raw cotton.

Nina Davenport could sew the wing back on
a butterfly, make them rise, cocoon, bloom
again. On every arm of every chair in the old
home house, her linen butterflies fluttered, her
needles pursed a power.

Lying there now is mean aunt Nina,
who won't die.

Nina, the general. Sergeant Maiden of the farm,
distributor of all good back breaking work
within a five-mile radius. Mean Nina, devoted
sister of Daisy, the sweet. I lift the sheet to see
what lies left of you. What shakes out is one
long as me crooked trembling bone.

You are without clothes from the waist down.
The diaper stamped "Large Adult." A middle
passage insignia. My eyes run headlong into
a summer afternoon shower. Wet, they whisper,
"Don't keep me here this long."

I cover back up the protruding pelvic bone that was
once your Black woman's saucy hip. I keep my hand
on you posting family messages through my fingers
all along your body board.

They never touch you here. They change your diaper
when they please, and their latex hands rake your
Indian hair, with what should be saved for mules,
archaeological digs.

I look inside your table drawer. The soft brush that
mama brought Thanksgiving Day is gone, disappeared
with all the other nice things. I turn to stampede the
office like all the other times before.

I want to know how they can steal from a woman
who won't die but your eyes fall on me like a shaft,
"Don't child, you get to go and I get to stay. You
don't know the half of mean when nothing but your
mind can leave the room."

She tells me there is good news. Insist I take word of
it back to the family. How she is no longer the meanest
woman in the world. She says the new night nurse,
the one called *Little Mary*, is.

Little Mary, who never looks me in my eye.

Every time she comes into the room aunt Nina stops
whatever she is saying, turns her voice into a needle,
searching for the jugular of *Little Mary's* ear,
"One day you will be old. You will."

All day she thinks and stares. Rolled up fetal, unable
to go anywhere except in her head. Every day staring
down the wall as it grows from dark to light. No corn
to shuck. Page to turn. Thread end to lick.
She remembers how mean to everyone she was.

"Mean Nina," mama and the rest of us whispered
every time the car pulled into the yard, before walking
into her house of butterflies and fresh pole beans.

That was when Nina Davenport could walk away
from you with great purpose. When everybody
thought she would just die easy, like the rest of us.
Teacher. Farmer. Spinster.

She surprised everybody and married a short man
once. The land needed a man's back for a whole season
and all the other hired hands had escaped one
night or another. Eventually he fled too.

That Sunday the new pastor said, "Meanness never
wears down easy." With his hand pummeling the
gospel plow, "Meanness," he swore, "can last longer
than plastic."

I grew up scared of her. But that was before, when I
thought she would just die regular. Back then I
would fly out of her way like a biddy in a barnyard.
Now that she is flat on her side, buckshot like a red
fox, I stand as close as I can, amazed that something,
finally, laid her meanness down.

Little Mary hates aunt Nina. On the outside Nina
Davenport is helpless. But on the inside she is whole.
Little Mary knows her body is bad but also knows
her mind is perfect. She hates her because aunt
Nina won't go on and go.

Because the other ones always give up easy,
die quick.

On Sundays aunt Nina prays out loud for lightning
to come, to strike them all down. She clarifies, this
is not further evidence of more meanness, just
everlasting belief in the power of prayer. There are
many kinds of believers.

Whenever Queen Mary enters the room she walks
right over and closes the drapes first thing.

Aunt Nina's forty-year teacher's pension pays the
bill each month. She doesn't care about the money
going up like smoke, only about the giving up,
of them winning. She says her bones are completely
castor oil now. She says this proud, like a soldier still
cleaning her gun between battles.

When I stand there beside her she recites Robert
Frost, summons the battle of Fort Sumter, remembers
the capitals of all the states. She asks me to sing them
back to her. I know she is memorizing herself back
to life.

She mumbles out recipes that won't work without
fresh churned butter and the twenty-nine places on
five hundred acres where she planted heirloom pears
that still pop out and fall to the red ground, her
hands no longer caramel cupped doilies, saving them
from the rabid ground worms.

Then, there are all the names, of all the neighbors
come and gone. Then, every year of every flood and
which house it took down what river. Then, which
summer the tornado laid every body down in the
snake ditch like pine board, one crooked row of
outstretched prayers, a family of drenched sin rising
finger first to the crazy sky.

Her mind perfect,
her body dead.

Here at the end she only wants one thing. She asks if I've remembered to bring it. I reach into the bag and sit it on the night stand. Aunt Nina strains her eyes to see.

I tear off the wrapper. I hold it out for her long inspection. She inhales, sighs, is so disappointed. "It used to smell meaner than that." She runs her fingers across the slippery sunken word, LIFEBUOY.

I warm the face cloth and slowly wash around her neck, sockets, temple. She quivers when I touch inside her ears. Her nose widens, smelling salvation and her eyes close remembering something private, something I can never ever know.

I tell myself only this old soap and ninety years of mean can do this to a woman. Make her feel something so old, so new, here at the end. I dry her off easy with the good towel that mama gave me, then uncap the blue top off the white opaque jar.

She bends her nose my way to test, her eyes close while everything turns sepia. The Ponds cold cream covers my two pointing fingers like an old woman's icing. Her skin dines. I know that what I bring to her in my paper sack is her only pleasure, the way she remembers how not to die.

She turns her face up to me when I am finished. I rub around her tinted eyes again before I go. I know I am tending to the beveled glass of a razed cathedral. She touches my arm,

"I guess I got to pay for all them mean days?"

I lie. I say, "No mam."

The Running of the Bulls

"Buy all the land you can buy while you can. So you never have to work for a white man. Dickman already did that. Already hit him for you too."

After slavery there were other chains.
The South still rounded up Black men

who wouldn't look the other way,
drop eyes or chin,

pass or step aside,
be cheated.

Men who saw red every day,
infrared patches glaring off

the white shirts of white men.
Black men who raised families first

then their scale of justice fists,
run out of the South

into the mist of the North.
Uncle Dickman (with his blue-eyed self)

saw red everyday
and finally occaned a white man's face into it,

for cheating him of hard earned wages.
Uncle Dickman, strapped North, before sundown

underneath the belly
of a wagonload of pigs.

For fifty years Granddaddy's eyes lusted for land,
the morning paper, a hunter's inky den;

afterwards his daily bread of sermon sliced
in even loaves garnished on the sides

of oven warmed Sunday plates.

Elephantine

I rode the head of an elephant
around and around
the dime store parking lot,
my long colored legs
dug in behind
his huge floating ears.

His body hair prickly,
a carpet of black straight pins
sticking me in the soft
sockets of my skin.
The chain around his wide foot
scraping the concrete,
both of us trembling
to not be there.

I was seven,
the man below smiling,
his long tall stick
writhing in the air
a charming snake.
Mommy said
I should ride the elephant
because traveling shows
didn't come our way often
and might never again.

You'll always remember this,
she promised.

The elephant shuffled beneath me,
his body crying as loud for home
as mine for ground.

This is all that remains
from a girl of seven,
everything else shattered now
broken into fragments
gone the way of pigtails,
presidential assassinations
and Black power movements.

Tonight on the news:
South African baby elephants
stripped of their mothers
and acacia trees,
waiting to be shipped
to more circuses and zoos.

Shackled just above their new knees,
they hobble about in tiny pens
until feet suddenly begin to move
like the fins of a huge land fish,
something acacied has just
crossed their inner eye.

Without warning one of them
pushes away from the fence,
flings her ton of memory into the air
and tries to catch it with her trunk;
burning to feel it again
what it's like to be elephant.

She bolts straight across
my dime store parking lot,
her diamond-cut ears flap and flail,
the hairy straight pins prick,
and I swat the back
of seven-year-old legs,
You'll always remember this,
comes across my headset,
I cup my ears
as she hits the electric wire.

The Undersea World
of Jacques Cousteau

The summer of '63
and I am only one Black girl
who belongs to the South.

A privileged one
who gets to walk to church
then mosey back home alive
without the pin of a bomb
clasped in my hair.

I am tiger eyed and sandy haired
and never afraid to jump
in the deep end of the city pool.

Men of all colors are being shot
like ducks on the wall
of America's country fair.

And the small eyes in my mama's house
are not allowed to watch T.V. news
but from the first we are encouraged to swim.

My grandmother tells me that in every
body of water deep enough to drown
there are people we know. She says
I should learn to swim, eyes open.

My fried bologna sandwich
has been eaten in the round.
A glass of Nestles chocolate milk
is one-half empty. I am spooning
leftover chocolate sludge up
from the bottom into my mouth
like sand candy.

My library books have been read;
they sit inside a Piggly Wiggly bag
rocking on the back door, waiting
to be returned.

I know I only have 28 minutes
before Mama pulls into the yard
sees me idle and leaps into her arias:

Why haven't you finished?
How was your spelling bee today?
Come help me with these beans.
Remember, I'll have no lazy daughter
living in this house.

I slide over to the wide glass box
that sits just off the floor,
one side houses Daddy's jazz records
the other says RCA Victor.
I turn the knob even though
there's not enough time.

My cars cup around the driveway,
my fingers go right to work,
it takes a long time for the light
to magically burst into form.

I push away, dragging my long body
back across the linoleum.
All my life I've been warned
about being too close to things.

But even at this young age I realize
I am five parts water, three parts magnet,
and positively electrical
about the things that matter most.

The screen door is closed,
the wooden one open,
it's not supposed to be
but I like things unshut.
I can see the yard,
hear Mama's Buick coming,
the soprano crickets are early.

A neighbor passes easy through
the hole in the back fence,
raising his right arm in a half wave
he moves through our part into his,
he doesn't stop to notice who's inside.

Living or dead he understands
someone is there.
This is the kind of respect
I grew up with.

My head turns back to the RCA Victor.
A man comes into view,
pushed there by all the waves.

He is sitting on the edge of a boat
named *Calypso*. I like the name.
He looks like some kind of hybrid fish
or tired seabird. I angle my head sideways;
I have never seen a white man like him before.

It is 1963 and I am a Black girl
in the South. One thing is for certain:
I do not trust white men.

I know them as creatures
who throw smoking things,
hide their many hands, disappear
out of sight.

A salty sea air is coming through
the old RCA Victor now. I inhale,
sit up straight, forgetting about Mama
and the time.

He is there again, an old white man
in a tiny red bathing suit no bigger
than a smile. There is something
watery about him that makes me
not turn away.

I laugh at his tiny bathing suit,
notice his arms moving like propellers.
He is dramatic.

I try out his language. A Black girl
from the waters of South Carolina
suddenly speaking a salty French.

I repeat the words as if I've said them
all my life. English appears down low
on the screen.

Every living thing needs water.

The interviewer explains
the seabird man's invention
and what a special moment
this is for the world.

We are about to go beneath,
to a place most have never seen before,
the Aqua Lung, a diving saucer machine
will take us there. I like seeing things
that no one has ever seen before.

I ignore everything that has ever
been told to me about being too close
to things electric and move in.
I am inches away from a screen of waves.

He takes one backward splash
that is so close that I reach and wipe my face.
Soon we are inside its belly moving along
wondrous spidery walls.

The old man's eyes swim soft and wild
behind a glass mask. I try out the words
of my newest language:

etoile de mer
tortue de mer
corail
oursin
algue

I disobey the haunting of southern
Black girl routines and practice
his every word,

Bienvenue dans l'ocean Atlantique.

We are speaking the same language now
a dialect of water and salt.
I am frozen on his wavy channel,
the seawater in me swelling.

I am more Atlantic than anything,
having been born there, right between
its lips, still having people, four-hundred-year-old
cousins, never met, still there.

I do not yet know who this man
wearing two smiles is. He is so slight, awkward,
chalky white, so comforted by my sea.

We have nothing in common except this
wet salty place where suddenly I realize
we both are from.

I think to myself: What if tomorrow,
on their way to work, all the white men
in the world dropped themselves over
the sides of their boats,
I might get to know them too.

Mama has pulled the Buick all the way in,
and cut its trembling engine. I reach and turn
off the RCA Victor, before he pulls himself
all the way out the water.

My fear: once out of the sea, he will be
just another white man rising from the depths,
a land creature once again able to hurl
sizzling rocks and words, fire his gun
then hide his hand so well. These ones,
their faces always cloaked in the
catastrophic language of divide and conquer.

Cousteau pulled me into the old water,
took me to see his violent peaceful planet.
He as fragile as it. We as vulnerable
as anything new.

Where always I felt more protected
than on any bloody land
ever walked beneath the confederate flag
of South Carolina
in 1963.

Ain't Too Proud to Beg

Ho Chi Mingh
And my father
Chain smoked
Salem cigarettes
All their lives;
I am my father's
Manifesto,
His little red book
Begging him to stop.

Hurricane
Beulah

Chapter One
Counting Straws

My grandmother is here visiting. This morning while she was still asleep on her back I crept up close and counted them all again. I've been studying Beulah Davenport's chin hairs for years now, hoping to know something about her powers. She has 19 chin hairs which are sometimes there and sometimes not. I stand in the doorway watching her in the bathroom mirror surrounded by Pop Leo's things; his razor and cup always on the side of the face bowl. Eventually, she will smooth pearl white lather down around her chin. Suddenly she is a tiny Black woman Santa, a caramel colored 'I Love Lucy' in classic pose, all in one. I like to watch as her 99-year-old hands move sideways across and under the belly of her barely wrinkled face. She does not see me leaning into the door wishing she wouldn't shave away her golden woman chin straw. *This is my research material!* I want to scream. She does not know that I believe these hairs hold the key to all her powers. She never sees me counting, pulling, on the tiny hairs beneath my own chin, wondering when, when can I count on being just like her?

Chapter Two
The Shopping Spree

(1)

This morning at breakfast we had an argument about putting the cans and bottles into the recycle bin instead of the trash can. She refuses to do it. I keep going behind her retrieving the shiny see-through things from the garbage. Yesterday she told me that only white folks save bottles and cans. She says Black folks save the earth just by getting up in the morning and deciding to go on one more day. *Yes mam*, I answered. I tell her I want to buy her something new for her 100th birthday. I ask her will she go to the mall with me to help me find it. She cuts off my sentence as soon as she hears the word *mall*. She says in her most amazed voice that she just heard on the radio that it's Senior Citizen's Day at the Salvation Army thrift store. She says, *Can you believe it, everything with blue and yellow tags is 50% off!* Already she is reaching for her pocketbook and slipping it on her arm and handing me my keys that I do not remember asking her for.

(2)

I am sitting at a four dollar desk at the Southside Salvation Army thrift store biding my time by writing poetry. It is badly stained and wobbly—not the poetry, I hope, but the desk. Every now and then somebody walks by and kicks the legs of it like it is a car they might want to take home. Just in the nick of time, I manage to raise my writing hand in the air, then wait for the table to stop shaking, as they decide whether they want it or not. Eventually, I go back to my writing. I've only had to change tables three times. Every now and then I look up from my writing to find my grandmother teetering down a row of color-coordinated clothes. She is moving now like an old Loggerhead trying to decide where best to lay her eggs. She is holding on to her walker, which along with her hearing aid she hates to use in public. At the same time she is pushing a rickety shopping cart. I don't know how she is doing both these things at the same time but she is. She is definitely one part magic. Every time I ask her does she need my help she sucks her teeth real loud and moves on up the aisle away from me, blues singing something about, "Don't treat me like I'm old, treat me like I can be recycled, remember."

(3)

She is up in aisle seven. She is carefully putting two- and three-dollar dresses into her push basket. Some of them I can see are expensive tweed and gabardine suits that I imagine rich ladies gained weight and outgrew. Some of them, I imagine, those same rich ladies might have worn up until their last day on earth. I imagine their children have brought these and others of their things here to the Salvation Army thrift store, no longer able to set a watery eye on them.

My grandmother is pulling out the most expensive things. When she holds them up for her inspection, looking for moth bites or broken zippers, I tell myself that I can see the outlines of the bodies of the women who once owned them still in them. Finally, I understand, this is the poem I want to write.

(4)

All of a sudden I am happy, finally I am thinking metaphorically. I start to wonder; what if the life we lived, all our days, was able to bleed into the fabric of our favorite skirt or dress. I imagine that I can tell which clothes in my grandmother's arms belonged to Black women and which did not. I stop writing and watch her more carefully. Every time she lifts something I whisper, "Yes mam, that one," or, "No mam, not that one." Every time I say, "No," this is the one my grandmother puts back on the rack. I am not crazy enough to think her secret powers allow her to hear me. I am crazy enough to know we think alike about some things. I believe when she holds each garment up she too can see the pain and scars, the broken dreams, disappointments and heartaches that she knows to be the map of too many of the lives of Black women she has known and been.

(5)

She puts these particular dresses, the ones that Black women must have owned, back on the rack as if they are made of stained glass. She touches them with a patient tenderness I rarely see in her anymore. I think her lips are moving as she does this. I believe she is saying, *Sorry Sister Girl, I don't need no more of that in my life. Done my time with all that. The only thing I want from clothes for the rest of my life is for them to be pretty or warm.*

I look away from her and notice all the brown and white and Black people moving into the store suddenly. They are coming and going down every aisle in families and groups. I look at my watch, it is just after five o'clock. Quittin' time. Dreamin' time out in the real world. Everybody looks tired. But I notice something so clear. As they come in, in their different coming-in ways, they all seem so excited. Excited to be in the Salvation Army thrift store. Maybe they believe they are standing in a place that holds the promise of things affordable.

(6)

My grandmother startles me by walking up in my blind spot on her way over to the fifty-cent glasses. (She says she needs more even though her kitchen cabinet won't completely close because of the two hundred already there.) She doesn't stop, she even crashes softly a few times into the old couches and floor lamps, saying as if they can hear, "Well, excuse me!" She turns to me before she is out of range again. "I do hope you are paying attention because everything you need to know about recycling, about what to save and what to throw away in your life is right here." She wobbles off down the aisle giggling to herself and running over everything in her way.

Chapter Three
The Bra

(1)

My grandmother is four foot eleven and some change. er 99-year-old body is a small work of art to me. Her Vaseline massaged skin is only now just starting to sag. She has never had much for hips. Her breasts are small but still fierce in their own way. More and more her back is bending in like a tiny mountain giving way to that pounding sea called old age. I am five foot eleven and a quarter with breasts enough for the whole family. Everywhere she is small boned I am big. She is maybe a hundred pounds, if you pour two oceans in her pocket, and I never go anywhere near bathroom scales anymore. This morning is the last full day of her visit and this morning I could not find my sports workout bra. The comfortable one with no underwire that doesn't poke me out like Miss Perfect Body in the Victoria's Secret commercial.

(2)

I am here with her at the Salvation Army thrift store again. This is our third straight day of shopping. We have been here for five hours already with no lunch bell in sight. She knows she is leaving tomorrow and so unlike all the other days she is stopping everybody in every aisle talking to them as if she will never see them again. She is acting like all weekend she has been attending some grand convention of little old lady Salvation Army shoppers and today will be the closing festivities. Also, she is treating the clothes unusually bad; stepping on them and sometimes even throwing them over the dusty splintered top of the door. I have been following behind her like a human vacuum cleaner. Occasionally, she wobbles up to the front counter in between trying things on, breaking in line ahead of others to remind the cashier that it is criminal to ask two dollars for a wool suit that has faded from pink to peach.

(3)

The people who work here have begun to smile at me. Some even make it a point to touch me on the shoulder when we pass in the aisle. One even whispered yesterday, "I could never do what you are doing." Today somebody passed by as I sat back down at my poetry table, "I could never have the kind of patience that you have." I smile back at them, too polite to say what I want to say, which is, *But this is my grandmother and I am 42 years old and she is 99 and we are here on earth at the same time. And I am all of who I am because she made me fried corn and cabbage every summer day that I lived with her as a child. And every time I entered her house as a girl there were homemade whole wheat breadsticks and apple fritters cooling on the side of the stove. There was blackberry juice waiting in mason jars that had already been tendered with the natural sugary spoons of her hands.* I want to say, *if you could still look up in the world and still see yourself in the eyes of the one who is the very reason you are still graciously free of madness, then you would do whatever you had to do for her.*

But all that's private so I go back to looking down the rows. Somebody I don't know sees me searching and points to the dressing room area as if they know who I must be looking for. I just smile and thank her with a nod of my head.

(4)

There are only two tiny dressing rooms. There are people waiting in a line to use them. There are lots of people waiting in line. My grandmother has made one of them her home away from home. Her movements are pretty slow. It takes her a long time to pull each dress down around her. My job is to return anything she does not want to the racks. She does not allow me to help her dress or undress. I reach to tap on the left side door because walking towards it I notice a hundred dresses already on the floor. I can hear my grandmother shouting through the door at the line of people telling them to be nice, "In Jesus name be nice!" She even counsels them through the door that they might consider leaving and trying the other Salvation Army thrift store on the west side of town if they are in such a hurry. I have no idea how she knows about the other store. I smile and back away from the line of people standing before the dressing room doors. I pray that they have grandmothers at home.

(5)

I pop my head inside Dressing Room Number One. She is there with a jungle of tops and bottoms and a sea of chiffon all around her feet. Just as I am about to take an armload of clothes back outside past the mob of waiters, I look at her and there is my lost sports bra. It is double wrapped around her small upper body like a body bandage. It is twisted and looped all around her like a bad seat belt that has been in several accidents. Somehow it is holding everything on her in; womanly, tight and youthful. I start laughing and the clothes start falling and she starts swatting me with a blue sear sucker jumper. "Something must be mighty funny for you to keep that door open so long for to give me The Pneumonia."

I stop laughing long enough to point to her upper body and she finally looks down at herself. She pokes up real close to the looking glass, straightens out her trifocals, leaning even closer to the mirror. It all comes into focus for her. "Lord Baby, that's why everything fittin' me so good today." We are laughing harder than we have ever laughed before.

(6)

As we exit the store the clerks are still shaking their heads. The manager passes by saying, "I have never seen two like you before." I know he has never seen two like us before. Because there has never been one like her before. One tall. One short. One fifty-seven years older than the other. The little girls inside us both still so pristinely intact and falling more and more in love with each other even as we grow older by the day and our bodies prepare for recycling, to say their goodbyes, but not our hearts, never our hearts.

Chapter Four
The Cancer

(1)

I am my grandmother's oldest granddaughter. Right from the start we knew we belonged to each other. On October 16th in the last year of all those 9's and six months after we left our twin mark on the Southside Salvation Army thrift store in Kentucky I drove all day to be with her in the land of our birth, South Carolina. For several weeks I had been driving home every weekend, we didn't know when or how or if. The doctor said "three months" but Ma Bea said *only God could know that.* When I walked in the door mama said, *She's been waiting for you and only you.* I walked over to the bed. She looked at me then turned away disgusted at not being able to reach for me or command her physical body with the precision that she had for 99 years. She could no longer speak but I knew she knew I was there.

(2)

For some reason her feet wouldn't stay under the bed cover. For two hours I held her right foot in my left hand and her left foot in my right, warming them with my body. Her little legs were still powerful and pumping so hard. Once she almost pushed me back against the wall. She seemed to be trying to run away. That's when mama said what almost broke my water, "Look at us, three generations of woman." I raised my eyes to the ceiling and pushed the rising salt back down. Ma Bea was staring at me, still hard and hopeful. Mama said the nurse had just left. She had put a brand new pain patch on her arm and whispered that Ma Bea's esophagus was now no bigger than a straw. I listened to her raspy rattling breath, watched her labor for every inhale. She stared at me like she was waiting for me to help her as I always had. I kept kissing her hands, humming back the salt, rubbing her feet and talking to her. Out of Ma Bea's direct sight mama started to shake.

(3)

In May when we received the diagnosis, we decided as a family to take care of Ma Bea in her own home. I moved in and lived with her over the summer and then mama came and stayed when I went back to teaching. As the cancer took more and more of her body away mama waited on Ma Bea with a brilliant seamless devotion.

(4)

They say that a daughter comes through the belly of her mother but through the spirit of her grandmother. Standing there before them both I realized this was the roundest moment I would ever know. I had no children. But my mother had become my grandmother's mother and I had become mother and daughter to them both. All our female lines and edges had disintegrated. I stared at mama. Her soft face was starting to show the wear and tear of both loss and birth. I knew better than to look towards the mirror.

(5)

A new kind of recognition was settling in now. Mama began
whispering two things back and forth to all of us standing there
in the room. She flipped desperately through the pages of the
Blue Book that the hospice nurse had left for us to reference in
her absence. "I've never seen her do this before," she said
nervously. "Do you think this is it?" My hands kept going from
my grandmother to my mother who sometimes fell on her knees
beside the bed in prayer when she got no earthly answers to her
questions. Ma Bea's legs were still full of great motion. Arms
and feet moving strong and fast. She was unable to control them
but she was still so willful. So determined to not go, even on this
last journey, without a fight. She wanted to tell us something
but nothing was able to exit her mouth anymore. I kept reassuring
her that I could hear her and in a way I could. My hands cupped
tight around her feet could hear her trying to run, could feel her
trying to tap out final instructions.

(6)

At 8:50 she stopped blinking her eyes. At 8:57 she took a
breath so deep it seemed to stop the clock that Mama was watching.
At 9:03 her beautiful pretty ankles went quiet in my hands and
she finally stopped trying to run. My salt blocks cracked wide
open. Family slowly encircled the bed.

(7)

*After wide hugs and great tears I searched the dresser tops and
drawers in my grandmother's bedroom but found none.* I finally
asked my uncle if he had any pennies on him. He reached into
his pocket and pulled out two brand new 1999 copper suns. After
daddy said the prayer and brother No. 1 crossed her arms across
her chest I kissed the pennies then closed down the eyes of the
woman who had taught me how to see.

(8)

The funeral home came at midnight. My father and my brothers carried Ma Bea out of her old home house and into the back of the loneliest car in the world. Daddy said it was tradition. He said, *We carry our own as far as we can.* As they passed by us in the yard my hands reached to touch the corners of the ocean blue velvet coverlet that draped her.

After the car pulled off I was unable to sleep. I stood there on the porch for hours. In my mind I kept seeing the long car moving off down the small dark street away from all of us. The wind started to pick up stronger by the minute. At two that morning the winds of Hurricane Irene hit South Carolina. I was still standing on the porch when everything started to bend down low. I hadn't heard the news about the coming hurricane. But in that goodbye moment nothing seemed out of the ordinary.

(9)

I was my grandmother's heart. We belonged to each other. She had taught me to believe in things unseen. Even before the long car was out of sight I was there on the porch waiting for a sign from her that she was alright. Standing there in the middle of her ocean of brilliant pansies and begonias, I watched pine and oak sway like summoned dancers then bend loyally like servants. And just before the birth of her favorite time of day, with a soft suddenness, I felt the warm heavy wind of the Great Mother lift the plain dutiful life of another mother to the beyond.

"I wish I could put my arms around my people and fly away."

~ Ida B. Wells Barnett

The Greatest Show on Earth

*For Saartjie Baartman, Joice Heth, Anarcha of Alabama,
Truginini, and us all.*

Under glass and tent
floating in formaldehyde jelly
curled in a deadman's float
live the split spread
unanesthetized legs
of Black women
broken like the stirrups
of a wishbone,

somebody got their wish
and somebody didn't.

The lilac plumage
of our petaled genitalia
in all its royal mauve
and plum rose
with matching eggplant hips
that pull the ocean
across itself each night,
boats of peanut skin
folded and rolled
like the new fur
all proof of our pathology
all cut away
by pornographic hands
fascinated with difference
and the spectacle
of being a Black woman,

so the normal pay their fifty cents
to see what makes a freak a freak.

Go ahead,
walk around her
she won't bite,
she is the headless woman,
see her protruding mass,
steatopygia.

We don't have to be dead first
to be cut into manageable size,
one that fits their measuring rods
their medicine chests will not rest
until we are properly pried,
it has always been about
opening us up,
experimenting with Black women
but never dissecting their own desires.

The side show
was pitched on our backs,
the speculum hammered out
between our legs,
modern medicine was founded
on the world of our hips;
we the standard patterned girth
of every bustle skirt ever made.

Black woman as spectacle,
wanting to but afraid to die.
Knowing death would never end
such sterling silver lust.
Bodies quake whole lifetimes
in a national geographic tremble
until the obituary arrives:

Please bury me behind the mountains
So they can never find me again.

But they do find us,
do dig us back up,
retrieve the last swatches
of soft skin,
the last twig of curved brown bone.

Our opened pirouetting vaginas,
our African music boxes
whittled down to perfect
change purse size,

for the normal
who will always pay
their fifty cents
to be sure and see
what makes a freak
a freak.

Shark Bite

Some things should never be eaten
or held anywhere near the mouth,
even when served in the best restaurant.

A germ of history
400 years old
can enter the meat,

even when exquisitely seasoned,
perfectly cooked, the chef award-winning,
the cutting board bleached daily.

In celebration of something forgotten now
I ordered shark for the first time
and my belly remembered what I had not.

Cannibal suddenly to my own history;
one dark, beautiful, devoured human being
going down my pipes like a chunk of lye,

made to straighten hair, not intestines.
Her scream hit the bottom of my belly lining,
her legs stretched out behind her

as if ninety days in the gut
of a slaver's ship was long enough

to be bent in a circle like a closed padlock,
suddenly in me she needed room
to stay alive.

She kicked with her long Black woman foot
and my fingers released the linen napkin
in my lap, touched for the hole in my middle,

and the delicious fish, the tender shark,
bloomed into a memory nova that
I did not know was there,

where there was a woman being raped
by nineteen men in shiny pilgrim shoes,

and the wondrous shark became
all 999 muscles of one brown man,
resisting his forced daily feeding again,

the whiskered fish was in the net of the schooner,
pulling down heavy in the middle, as an obedient
brown bean of a child was told one last time to

fly

later that night as I stooped over
trying one final time to bring it all up,
through a curtain chill of tears,

every delicious miserable bite
sixty million and more
hands wringing my stomach,

like dirty wash that wouldn't come clean.
I wrestled with sheets and pillow cases
and memory to find peace.

There was a ship,
the Henrietta Marie,
breaking against the furious water,

and there were shackles
and the woman on deck
her legs open in the hiss of a scream,

and the man refusing to eat or live
reaching for her
and the child finally flying,

and I was there
unfurling with them,

pushing my legs back
out of their comfortable
lady-like curl,
like a shark smelling water
in her blood.

Sign Language

For the man who jumped out in front of the woman with his
arm raised like a machete screaming **Abomination!** *as she*
walked the streets of San Francisco holding her lover's hand
for the first time in public.

There is a woman who goes to sleep
every night wishing she had broken
your sternum reached up inside your
chest momentarily borrowing your
heart to hold before your screaming
face and with her other hand still
clutching her lover's broke next into
her own sternum plucking next her
own heart dangling them both there
sterling silver sign language for you
tell me what is the difference.

The New Cotton

They are just boys, chain
ganged to the side of the road,
dressed to the nines in sunny
orange, that shade of red that
never seems to set, familiar
color of that foreign flower,
the kind you can close your
eyes in sleep and still see, but
these boys are not flowers
anymore, no
thing that can be seen to bloom
has been left to bloom, in this
place where a chain around a
Black man's ankle is the state
jewel, but if you still own your
eyes you know they are still boys.

They do not yet know how to
bend, someone has not yet
passed on the secret
of how to save their backs
for the rest of the journey,
someone forgot to offer the
old way of how to get through
the whip of their young days
in order to reach the sweet
rock of their old, they angle
and arc carelessly, not knowing
they are match
sticks of American history,
never squatting down low
in the grass, never bending
at the ankle or thigh, they are

such proud brittle lion trees
about to break in every
direction but free, the weave
of all their fabric wasted
in the constant picking up
of useless plastic things,
that as I get closer,
that as I pass,
look white and sticky plump,
some kind of new cotton
stuck inside their reaching
Robeson hands.

The Girlfriend's Train

"You write like a Black woman who's never been hit before."

I read poetry in Philly
for the first time ever.
She started walking up,
all the way, from in back
of the room.

From against the wall
she came,
big coat, boots,
eyes soft as candles
in two storms blowing.

Something she could not see
from way back there but
could clearly hear in my voice,
something she needed to know
before pouring herself back out
into the icy city night.

She came close to get a good look,
to ask me something she found
in a strange way missing
from my Black woman poetry.

Sidestepping the crowd
ignoring the book signing line,
she stood there waiting
for everyone to go, waiting
like some kind of Representative.

And when it was just the two of us
she stepped into the shoes of her words:

Hey,

> *You write real soft.*
> *Spell it out kind.*
> *No bullet holes,*
> *No open wounds,*
> *In your words.*
> *How you do that?*
> *Write like you never been hit before?*

But I could hardly speak,
all my breath held ransom
by her question.

I looked at her and knew:
There was a train on pause somewhere,
maybe just outside the back door
where she had stood, listening.

A train with boxcars
that she was escorting somewhere,
when she heard about the reading.

A train with boxcars
carrying broken women's bodies,
their carved up legs and bullet riddled
stomachs momentarily on pause
from moving cross country.

Women's bodies;
brown, black and blue,
laying right where coal, cars,
and cattle usually do.

She needed my answer
for herself and for them too.
Hey,

> *We were just wondering*
> *how you made it through*
> *and we didn't?*

I shook my head.
I had never thought about
having never been hit
and what it might have
made me sound like.

> *You know how many times I been stabbed?*

She raised her blouse
all the way above her breasts,
the cuts on her resembling
some kind of grotesque wallpaper.

> *How many women are there like you?*

Then I knew for sure.

She had been sent in from the Philly cold,
by the others on the train,
to listen, stand up close,
to make me out as best she could.

She put my hand overtop hers
asked could we stand up
straight back to straight back,
measure out our differences
right then and there.

She gathered it all up,
wrote down the things she could,
remembering the rest to the trainload
of us waiting out back for answers.
Full to the brim with every age
of woman, every neighborhood
of woman, whose name
had already been forgotten.

The train blew its whistle,
she started to hurry.

I moved towards her
and we stood back to back,
her hand grazing the top
of our heads,
my hand measuring out
our same widths,
each of us recognizing
the brown woman latitudes,
the Black woman longitudes
in the other.

I turned around
held up my shirt
and brought my smooth belly
into her scarred one;
our navels pressing,
marking out some kind of new
equatorial line.

Hate

Arthur Ravenel, Republican Senator from South Carolina, called the NAACP the "National Association for Retarded People" at a confederate flag support rally. He later said, "I made a mistake and I feel badly about it because I said 'retarded people' and I have a retarded son." He added, "That does not mean I'm apologizing to the NAACP."

How does a father
with a son struggling
to be seen whole
in the eyes of the world
forget the son long enough
for a slip of the tongue
to be recorded forever
for posterity's sake.

How does a father think
that a son will never know
what he said that day at the rally
when he slipped
and he the father revealed
his true feelings
about he the son
the same feelings he feels
about other different people.

How does a father
slip off one tongue
while he is rallying
his confederate troops
and slip on another
later
after the rally
when he is home

with his son
gentle inheritor of his name.

He does not.
The slippery tongue
is one and the same.

What could make you
forget your son?
A fight over a flag?
The heat from a simmering
hundred-year-old war?

Hate stops at nothing.
Not even the sacred door
to a son's private room.

Easy Bake

"Go home and tell your daughters they are beautiful."

~Stokely Charmichael

Every day there are more sightings,
children latched to guns are in this year.
School shootings all the rage.

Especially young girls who don't want
to be girlfriends anymore. They, the widest
target, the largest pile of bodies.

White boys with high powered rifles shirk,
take position behind flowering trees, the birthday
bow still tied in a knot at the trigger, their sites
set on the whole school yard, the whole prayer
circle.

In the crosshairs, flipping back and forth,
is it a deer grazing peacefully, or a little girl
saying *No*.

Across town, Black boys prefer close range,
hot pistols no bigger than their hands burn
their six-pack stomachs, they call out another
Black boy's name, *On your mark, get set,*
bitch.

In the news this morning, right beside
the most recent school shooting, advertisements;
toy easy bake ovens umbrellaed with the caption,
"What Every Little Girl Wants!"

My eyes zoom in back and forth.
The bodies of the girls are rolled out
covered in white sheets, a mother is
screaming her way through the crowd.

Inside the doors of those easy bake ovens
I imagine a place for bulletproof shields.
Something for the unspoken, for after
we teach our daughters to cook, clean and
walk two steps behind any man,
as long as he is that.

I imagine a matching ensemble, an easy bake
vest and shield; so that they may defend themselves
from what we are teaching our sons.

Labor Strike

Black girl
bobbin' on the Wednesday street,
McDonald's pencil
layin' back
'cross her ear,
like she ain't at work
and heretofore
from now on
for evermore
is refusin' to take
your orders.

My Old Kentucky Home:
Where the darkies are gay*

From the week of October 25, 1994, after the killing of 18-year-old Antonio Sullivan, shot in the head at close range by a policeman.

What I See: Shiloh Baptist Church

At the funeral, young Black men glide in,
still in school clothes. They file into the old
neighborhood church looking around like
strangers. Their books, folded and silent, sit
back behind them on wooden pews like the
bricks of a hundred frozen futures.

A steady stream of boy-men wet down
every aisle. They lean into the netted open
arms of each other. I notice, on them nothing
fits; their pants, their shirts, their fear,
everything is too big.

A domino of young men from every local
village, eyes bursting like tall hydrants, they
circle around his open casket, brown faces
shining, spotlights pointed, beating, lasered
toward him like the last resort of some kind
of power source.

They huddle, afraid of the death staring up
at them but they are more terrified of leaving
him there, alone, so they break the rules. They
linger and the service cannot start, not until
they sit. But they are hovering like a hundred
humps in a gigantic umbrella, his last protection.
We see the downpour begin. They stand so long
by his side, their ocean of eyes begging,
Wake up!

*Kentucky state song lyrics

They lean on his chrome baby-blue capsule.
They have their private conversations. One
of them, as if he has seen it done in a movie,
runs his long brown fingers in front of his
eyes just to make sure. A hundred lamp
posts all curving in to see what their eyes
cannot believe.

They make for him a silvery black moon
of themselves. They crescent a way into his
last earth memory. They greet him for the last
time in their tradition, by tucking things down
and under his cardboard body for his
final journey.

They put private male things all around him.
Things we can't see from our seats. It is an old
Affrilachian mountain custom, to put things
in the pocket of the young dead, it is done
in grand hip-hop style.

I want them to take off their hats in God's house.
This is what I want, what my mother and father
and grandparents would want. What others who
think they know what it is like to be Black and
young and male, raised on the east side of this top
100 mid-American city want, but this is not what
they do.

These invisible sons of invisible sons, these
grieving cornrowed eagles do not remove
their hats. They do turn the brims of them
around from front to back. (They have their
way and you have yours.) Finally they turn
and scatter out into the pews, by twos and
threes and tens, walking. They stumble into
the stark white light of T.V. cameras. But
what they are really blinded by is how
he did not get up this time, not this time.

The organ music takes over now. They walk
out like crippled men, so much slower than
before. These veterans of world wars, numbers
three and four, lift their heads. Anyone with
half a heart can see the birthmarks of grease
paint smeared across cheeks and chests. They
walk away, readying themselves for a life
of more war.

Life will not wait for them to finish their mourning.
It will call them back to the land of the living-dead
before they are ready. By the nape of their mother
given necks: Jerome, Earl, Robert, Willie Lucious,
Willie James Junior, will return to the front lines
alongside the ghosts of their fight-the-good-fight
fathers.

What I Dream: The Lexington Cemetery

When they run out of burial land (and they will
at the rate we are going) the already-dead will
be the ones who will save us. Those who have
been gone for a hundred years or more will be
the ones who will finally give us the life we don't
seem to know how to create.

Every set of bones over one hundred will be
moved to one mass grave site, set aside by the
Commonwealth. It will be commandment: All
must leave their private single dwellings and
be made to mix-mingle with others
unlike themselves.

It will be Law, passed by House, Senate
committee, Frankfort lobbyist, even crooked
good-old-boy Kentucky politician. They will
think they are saving precious, irreplaceable
bluegrass farms, but they will be saving more.
Henry Clay, statesman and winningest politician,
will lay beside Issac Murphy, statesman and
winningest jockey, and when the dust has settled
on that new day he will ask what he always
wanted to know, *What was it like to ride an
animal so fast?* And Murphy will answer,
Like signing the wind into Law.

Those dead, a hundred years or more, will just
be deemed "the expendable dead." They won't
be the Black dead or the white dead, the rich dead,
the poor or the revered. They will just be the dead.
We will have to do this because we will no longer
have the space to be as thoughtful about the dead,
because we have been so thoughtless about the living.

And so the salt trucks will move through
the award-winning Lexington cemetery
gathering up the bones of all centenarians.
The same trucks will cross the train
tracks and amble through the sacred overgrown
African graveyard #2, gathering up everyone
certified over 100 years. All will be moved

to the prepared mass grave that was once an old
horse farm. This will be the new law of the old land.

There won't be room to argue about it. Money won't
matter. Family stock won't change any minds.
It won't be a question of race or baptism, pedigree,
class or *Did your family buy or were they sold on
Cheapside Street?*

Black and white finally skinless and naked to the
bone will be taken away to live together and some
seventy-year-old youngster left standing on the
corner will say out loud as the salt trucks pull away,
*"Well I never thought I would live to see the dead give us
this day our daily bread."*

And there finally in the common denominator
of their hundred years of death, and by the common
denominator of the survival of the living, the fear
will be no more. Finally, white bones will fall and
snuggle up next to black bones and no one will care
or be able to tell who was ever who.

And the talking, save the hugging, that needed to
happen last week, light years before he shot him
and he fell dead and everybody who knew him
took to the streets hurting like hunger, while
everybody else hurled *Riot!* out into the autumn
wind like an aperitif.

Cheekbone to cheekbone up close, black femurs will
touch white metacarpals and white eye sockets will
soften back at black eye sockets noticing that they
once were blessed with sight but chose not to see.
Black shins will graze white shins, white funny

bones will even crook around black funny bones and laughter will roll in like a late train. Because the only thing left will be bones. No memory to pass, no skin to fear.

Dead folks long gone, without a memory to keep hate alive, without a mind to remind them of a racist word or deed, without a family trait, tradition, stereotype, hurtful dismissing glance, without skin to designate the racial tribe, will be left to create on this earth what we were supposed to be all along.

What I Think: The Press Conference

The year will be 2595. The archaeologist will read from his detailed report. He will be an incredibly well known theorist with a brilliant scientific mind, exact in his capacity to explain what life on earth was like in 1994, some 600 years before.

Just how did people live together on this land? This will be the hot topic of the day. He will stand before the floating computer monitor and report that even though it has been a two billion dollar, twenty-five-year study, there are still some unanswered questions: Like how the darker ones of the species (not all but certainly far too many for it to have been mere coincidence) and primarily the young adult males, had these strange holes searing some part of their craniums.

He will say his research shows that the holes were put there by some type of hunting invention and *We are still exploring how this condition could have been so prevalent.* He will add that just because

there is no reasonable explanation does not mean
there is no explanation at all.

He will recall several times during the report
that the society back then as a whole was highly
technologically advanced. He will say that it does
not really make sense. He will look perplexed, take
off his glasses and finally put his notes away. As
the news conference ends he will conclude his
findings:

It is all very strange to us. As strange as the other
finding, which we had not seen evidence of since
79 A.D., a continent away in the city of Pompeii,
where the mummified bodies of the smaller
children in the same housing structures as their
older siblings were found crouching in corners,
99% of whom seemed to have died with their mouths
wide open as if in the middle of one long unbroken
scream.

"It's not that complicated, but you're gonna need a bulletproof soul."

~ Sade

Afro-Gregorian Chant

The wild monks sing
and my fingers are pushed for good,

eight hours wafered,
the perfect food for the broiled toast

of your sleeping knees.
The great Smokey mountains

fall in on us,
Cherokee trees curl liquid smoke

and I am alone with the curve
of the road and a missing hand,

which now has fallen asleep beneath,
along with the rest of you.

This is the holiest of life.
The castanetting call of celibate men

frolicking the air,
Gregorian monks chant away spanishly

as the shawl of Appalachia is thrown
and you asleep through it all.

Missing the bloom of God in fall
and the salt of palmetto shores closing in.

As the sun bakes your face
through the tempered stained glass

into the holiday warm of pecan pie,
the soft mouths of chosen chanters

turn to wedding bells
while inside the pine

and the baobab
the everywhere eyes

of mere lovers
boil.

Frog Legs

In bed at night
the bottom half of her
never sleeps.

Her legs,
ocean tendril
of mad motion
even when the rest
of her
decides to call it
a day.

All day long
she has moved
through the world
a Black woman,
at night
she sleeps
like one too.

Restless,
on land
and sea.

Her beautiful
bouquet of legs
disregards the rest
of her higher education;
running her
in place,
spinning her
amphibiously
around.

Sex

*After being told, "Oh what would you know
about it anyway."*

How the room rained down
a mother's only blistering ash,
her words lifting then settling
clear and hot, then the branding
of me complete.

After she proclaimed
to the rest of the family
that whatever it is I do
with another woman
could never even-steven
to what she does with daddy.

As if my way to human pleasure
too inefficient to be called the same.
As if we who do with a woman
should find a new name
for the doing.

She, believing that my body
coming together with another
woman's a fake freak of nature,
not sex or love and could never be.

The sermon of her looks
always the same.

How my pot of woman
is not worth its salt
because there is not the pepper
of a man there.

That, in order for any woman
to cook up a thing worth
sensually serving
a lid and seasoning
of a certain fit and taste
is required.

That what I offer to the diamond
and life of another woman, that
then streams up my two front
female spines, that branches off
into a desert orchid, that grows
into a family of complicated
spiraly things in the middle
of any hot springs geyser night,
is not worth its weight in sweat.

As if what I know about pleasure
and the microscopic fittings of love,
about the filling of an appetite
that lives somewhere between
my cerebellum and my thigh tissue,
that runs like a southern railroad
trestle to my heart bone emptying
next into my lung sacs, as if that
tenderness which douses all the gates
of my body clean and wet like all
the steamed water and wind that
ever was in the world suddenly
let loose, as if what comes from
the zest and tongue of another
woman's capsule to my own;

that intricate complicated vessel
of how and what we shape our
loving into, cannot be compared
to what she has felt between her
own gulf stream.

Mama, what appears shut sky
to you, is heaven opened wide
to me.

The Turtle Suite Poems

I. The Dive

*"Okay, so you don't love me no more but I wish you well,
'cause there's enough misery in the world."*

~ *Curtis Mayfield*

The weight of the world is less underwater
As you leave I submerge   Begin the moving
Through   With everything unfinished between
Us   Hoisted high upon my back   Tied down
Like winter tinder   This the deep freeze dive
My green brown shell heavy   All the way to
The oval edge   With all I believed would
Always be   The salt water helps   Lifting all
Of it from me without taking anything away
The sweet scorched things still try to flee
Like a school of red bandana fish   The geechee
Blue wedding roof blown off in the storm   Rice
And popcorn   Piled high   Scattered out their
Smoldering bowls   Along with the most
Singed memory of them all   Your curtain of
Brown eyes opens   First thing in the blackberry
Morning   Sweet things bobble and put up a
Good fight   Refuse to fall   All treasures
From a shipwreck
Now piled high
Submerged now
Underwater now
The nest destroyed
The sharpest hook of all
Ruthless fire pirate
Love

II. Steamed Rice

"In me nothing is extinguished or forgotten."

~ Pablo Neruda

When we were married,
we always ate one bowl
of steamed rice first,
ritual appetizer
you said,
to clean
prepare
the mouth
for the rest of the meal
on the way.

> *Coming,*
> *pungent garlic,*
> *lilting scotch bonnet,*
> *circling behind us*
> *on the stove*
> *in a curtain of curling heat.*

Now that we are not,
I long for one bowl
of rice reversed
with steam enough
to pull your carpet
of chocolate pepper
from the roof
of my mouth.

"Where does a Black soul go to rest?"

~ *Randall Robinson*

Metallurgy

for Cassandra Wilson

She's the one who won't leave us.

She sings and cobwebs are strung
like salve, like liniment laced,
every note forging iron.

Her low sulfur notes swim
in a buttered brine. Her reddened mouth
parachutes around leaping Africans,
resuscitating the butterbean breath of Black boys.

She keeps bringing up the past
like it's a throat,
with a muddy Mississippi fish bone
stuck crossways.

At her Marian Anderson table we always eat our fill.

She opens like a furnace (all southern),
walks us to the flame (all polite),
refuses to enter the pretty waters of the melody
without the rest of the scorched story in tow.

She sees to the keeping of the shells,
studies the motions of Black mermaids;
draped in crepe myrtle,
waist high in red dirt octaves.
She learns it back to us
by way of the highway of the ear.

Before the end of the song;
we check our wrists,
we lick our lips,
we taste ankle iron.

She's the one who won't abandon.

On stage, under lights, she's slipping
through the thicket again, untying
grandmama's hands, every gnarled
throat in the room straightens, finally
free of scuppernong, wisteria.

She enters the room
and a valley of blackbirds takes off,
the furnace opens and closes
all the copper in us turns toward
the magnet of her breath.
Every penny we've ever saved
in mason jars, for the ritual closing
of the eyes, rattles.

Her coral indigo humming raises
adolescent cousins full term, pouring
salt into the historical wound. When
her eyes close on the clef of treble,
when her head goes back past the
beginning of hypnosis, she is seeing
things again.

The Atlantic ocean's greatest slaughter
is scribbled beneath her lids in
scarred black codes.

With or without guitar she can pluck you.

She enters counterclockwise
all the while in Ring Shout time
Slipping slew footed mildly like a monk,
round and round the floor
until gold is discovered
in the pan of her feet.
In half notes she flutters.

She's the one who won't leave us.

A girl from Jackson, from that place
where in concert daughters are raised
only once, given African guitars,
then taught the iron songs, instead of
bedtime stories, then set upon the world.

Songs that tell:
how never to leave,
how never to leave us,
how never to leave well enough alone.

Assam

Old Black woman heavyweight
body conscious now
after years of swinging
wide chocolate wings
below her waist
wedged now into the surf for good,
her treasures
sunk into the sand
of self consciousness.

From her throne
she watches more than moves
these days
I walk by noticing;
things still pull to her,
the uncalled water
knocks softly
bubbling about
her flat out thighs,
the wet salt wanting in,
no matter.

Her fingers disobey
the rest of her
and climb down.
Alone, they turn
into years
of summer grandchildren
running from the chasing water
straight into her netted arms.

She sits,
dripping
half in half out
the sea,
a tea bag full
of black uncut leaves,
without you I whisper
the world is plain
tap water.

A Hero Ain't Nothing
But A Sandwich*

In Atlanta,
two men and a high-rise building on fire.
The one building it, with his good hands,
still on top pushed into its last heavenly corner.

The other flies around, dangling from a rope
dropped from a helicopter, his good hands
desperately trying to reach.

One Black man, one white.

A tiny opening of air and the helicopter slips
through the smoke. They peel out their open arms.

One of them wraps his legs about the other.
It is a fireman's way of rescue.
In a loverly embrace they face each other
all the way back down to earth.

Once back on ground they are safe.
Life gets back to normal. But I'm not ready
for them to be safe and life as normal hasn't
worked in four hundred years.

Zoom the helicopter back up.
Lock their legs back tight around each other.
Let the sight of them clasped there like
question and answer something more than
accident.

Their bodies dancing down, their gallant
purple hearts staring, iris to slow-dragging iris.
Make the sight of that linger longer than highlights
on the nightly news.

*Title of Alice Childress novel

Not one more feel-good story about one more
local hero, patted on the back, only to be
forgotten, because he was only doing what he
was trained to do, nothing else.

But before they zoom back up, re-categorize it.

Call what keeps us from each other's arms
what it is. Call hatred by its name; A firestorm,
category one; the kind that burns whole countries
down.

And to whomever
is flying the helicopter with us all,
apologize for the inconvenience
but now you may announce
how none of us can come down
until it's
out.

The Making of Paper

for Toni Cade Bambara (1939 – 1995)

*In the early 80s, I spent two years in a writing workshop that Toni
Cade Bambara held in her Atlanta home. Anybody in the community
who was writing was welcome. I adored the opportunity to sit at this
great writer's feet who knew so much about so much. In 1990, she
moved to Philadelphia and was later diagnosed with cancer. We
talked on the long-distance line when we could. I would always ask
if there was anything she needed that I could send. She usually
answered no. But in our last conversation, which took place one
week before she crossed over, she held the phone a little longer.
"Maybe," she said, "maybe you could send some paper and what
about one of those fat juicy pens?"*

Imagine that,
you asking me for paper.

For the record let me state
I would hunt a tree down for you,
stalk it until it fell
all loud and out of breath
in the forest.

Much as I love a tree,
fat, tall and free.

As anti-violent and pro-vegetarian
as I am.
Never been much
for strapping a gun
to any of my many hips,
for any reason whatsoever,
but on the copper penny eyes
of my grandmother, I tell you
this: I would hunt a tree down for you.

And when found
I would pull it all the way down the road
through congested city streets all by myself
and deliver it straight away
to your hospital bed,
one single extra-large floral arrangement,
something loud and free,
with red and purple bow.

Or better yet,
this tree loving
gun hating Geechee girl
would strap a wild west
gun belt machete
around her hips
enter the worst part of the woods alone
and go trunk to trunk
until the right one appeared
growing peaceful in its thousand-year-old
natal pot.

Look it
right in its
round rough ancient eyes
and confess away,
tell it straight to its woody face,
my about to do deed.

I'd even touch it
on its limbs,
fingers begging forgiveness,
give as much comfort to it
as I could, while trying to
explain the necessaryness

of its impending death;
me standing there,
my *Gorilla My Love* eyes
spilling all over everything,
sending up papyrus prayers
that all begin with,
"I'm so sorry but Toni Cade needs paper."

Only then would I slash its lovely body
into one million thin black cotton rag sheets
just your uncompromising size.

Send you some paper?
Oh yes,
paper is coming Toni Cade
wagonloads
in the name
of your sweet Black writing life,
from Black writers everywhere
refusing to leave
the arena
to the fools.

Paper is on the way.

Fishing Among the Learned

(1)

On the banks of her butterfly pond
Grandmother would stand,
as fluid as a waterfall, teaching
with a Five and Dime pole in her hand,
Be still and listen to that,
she could be heard to say.

She would make more good decisions,
lose more control, gain, relinquish power,
care about more people, recycle energy,
discern more foolishness
in an afternoon of fishing
than Congress ever could
be they all Democrat, all Republican.

My first semesters ever were spent
staring up at this Human University,
shifting my weight from bamboo leg
to trout flat foot waving first cow fly
then firefly from off her apron dress,
listening to the sounds swelling
around us, there was noise, there
was instruction, there was a difference
in the two.

This kind of standing stare at still water;
Fresh Water Philosophy, this speaking on
the depths of a true life lived full; Saturday
Sociology, footprints baked into the soft
bank; Advanced Lucy Geography. These
outdoor lessons could go on for days and
did, as long as there was sun and bait there
was learning.

To educate means to lead out,
she whispered to me on the snakish road
home. I had no idea what she was saying
or why now.

At well lit nightfall in between the quiver
of country bugs I'd wonder why she'd stood
me there, that pole in my hand gripped tight
as teeth full born to a jaw insisting, *Girl,*
pond water is as good as any book.

She'd already said to me in dreams, *A good*
teacher can do more than talk about it, she
can see it beyond the convincing skinny pages
of any flattened tree.

There on that bank preparing me for giant
whales when she knew full well bream and
mullet were all we had tugging our lines.

You don't fish just to catch, you fish so you
can keep, so you can put something back,
the fisherwoman taught. *It has less to do*
with the fish and more to do with your line
staying in the water, with your hand on the
pole, with discerning rituals, sniffing out the
weather, with what you can figure out about
yourself that early in the quiet morning in
between the iridescent help of sun or moon,
in between the magnificent bites.

Know what you will not let corrupt you, that
you cannot be bought or sold, assume another
will come after you have gone, their own pole

tight in hand as well hoping to catch something.
Put something back whenever you can, then she'd
untie the hook from its mouth, lay it back
in the soft velvet water, her fingers already
asking forgiveness.

Now that is something to keep.

(2)

I cast out among the learned and teach
to alter sleeping states. I stand before the
university pond and fish for the living who
send air bubbles up to the learned who know
real life bestows no terminal degrees.
I have come to know that we all dangle here;
grub and silkworms alike casting out our
many different lines. The well baited and the
barely hooked while the new recruits watch,
the old sentries look out silently. We push away
from shore annually, calling our rolls like salmon
pole vaulting, determined to remember the old
ways to wisdom, do or die.

Fishing is the key to everything that moves.

A poet needs to fly fish in the middle of the
bluest grass in order to catch glimpses of
the privileged information; that there are too
many meetings and not enough conversations
going on. A poet needs to stand girded before the
listening eyes of those who pay their hard earned
money wondering, *Will I teach them anything that*
the world will later ask of them to be sure and know?

I must.

Inside the polished granite of Academe
a poet must hope beyond hope that we will
all keep fishing at the bank and one day forego
the carnivorous weigh-in, the comparison of
scales, and instead throw our prime catch back
while keeping the feeling of casting out close.

A poet invited to the marble table must cast out
a cat gut cord, a thousand pound live wire,
with hook enough for all and reel in everything
she sees and speak of the good with the bad
and hope for the best, do or die.

And cocoon along with the rest spinning for
silk, for sheepskin, for sanity, for something
higher, more enduring than sweet tenure
or paper trails, for the high and honored art
of teaching, of returning something real to the
mental food chain; to transform one single life.

I stand I cast I feel I fish for something
that lives here in these waters, something
some of us have hooked but most have never
pulled all the way to the surface, something
we'll eternally feel nibbling our lines but never
lay our eyes free and flat upon if we do not
study the scholarship of fishing.

(3)
In the spirit of the old blind ones, those who
would take their chances in a heartbeat, pull
up safe anchor, all their eggs trembling in one

basket, throw your line out a little farther
tomorrow. Remember their commandment;
"If you do what you've always done,
you're gonna get what you've always got."

Don't pull your line in too fast,
Grandmother would say out the corner of her eye,
Keep your hook in the water all the way to the edge;
that's where the great tadpoles swim.

There are possibilities all the way to the end,
whatever you do, take fishing with you.

The sound of air bubbles
and that of lips pursed
just below the surface of an idea
ready to bite, the bobber being pulled
down into the luminous murky world
of the imagination. Once airborne and
arcing the tiny mullet changing into the
giant Orca right before our very eyes.

Now that is something to keep.

Charm

The two of them
standing on the other side
of the airport window,
Mama wiping her eyes
and looking through her purse
for anything of hers
to lastly give.
Daddy with his hands
one hundred leagues deep
in his salty pockets,
his black pearls
already secretly handed over
earlier in the day.

The way they stand there
with nowhere else
to go or be,
two watchlights watching
until the last of me
is all the way out of sight.

Nobody waits like this anymore,
nobody loves this way anymore.

"Circle is never broken."

~ *Cassandra Wilson*

Nikky Finney was born in Conway, South Carolina in 1957 at the mouth of the Atlantic Ocean and is now the Associate Professor of Creative Writing at the University of Kentucky. During the 1999-2000 academic year, she was the Goode Humanities Professor at Berea College in Berea, Kentucky. Her first collection of poems, *On Wings Made of Gauze* (William Morrow, Inc.), was published in 1985. Her book *RICE* (Sister Vision Press, 1995), a collection of poems, stories, and photographs, was awarded the PEN American Open Book Award in 1999. In 1998, the University Press of Kentucky published *Heartwood*, a collection of short stories she wrote to assist literacy students across the country. Finney travels and reads her work the world over and is particularly inspired by working with community groups and young writers.